The Way Out

Shlonda Miller

ISBN: 978-1-961258-61-7

Dedication

For my beautiful daughters Shaniya and Kelis. May you always allow God to guide your every step and lead you back when you go astray.

Acknowledgment

I would like to express my gratitude to all of my life experiences for shaping me into the woman I have become. A special thanks to my parents for raising me to honor God always and for allowing me to learn the necessary life lessons for my growth. I appreciate all the tough love.

I am deeply thankful for my loving husband and my beautiful daughters who have always believed in me and pushed me to be my greatest self. Gratitude extends to all those who have played a part in my life journey, whether it was positive or negative. You have helped shape and mold me into who I am today.

I am also grateful to my writing team for their invaluable support in getting this story on paper. Your efforts are truly appreciated.

Thank you all.

Table of Contents

About the Author

Shlonda Miller, born in Texas in 1983, is a devoted wife and mother of two daughters. Alongside her roles in the family, she is a dedicated CEO and a current student at the University of North Texas, pursuing her bachelor's degree in applied arts and science. Shlonda is not only an alumna of Dallas College but is also currently working towards her second associate degree in science.

Preface

In the quiet corners of faith and the shadows of youthful curiosity, Shelly's story unfolds. Trapped within the confines of her disciplined household, her dreams of freedom found a flickering hope in the exciting life of her friend, Amaya. From the rigid structure of her parents' beliefs, she peeks into Amaya's world of parties and friendship, a life seemingly unreal to her.

Yet, as she stepped into the deceptive charm of rebellion, the colors faded into shades of despair. Entangled in the clutches of a toxic relationship, she discovered that liberation came at a grievous cost. Bruised and broken, Shelly embarked on a journey back to her parents, who loved her dearly.

Within their open arms, Shelly's tarnished spirit found a refuge. Her story is one of endurance, strength, and belief in God. It's a story of acceptance, repentance, and a young woman's struggle to rekindle her faith, find her way back home, and mend the fragments of her shattered soul.

Chapter One

"Yearning For Freedom"

The sunlight peeked through the stained-glass windows, casting colorful patterns on the worn wooden pews of the small church. It was a typical Sunday morning, and Shelly Winter, known to her friends as Shell, sat quietly in her usual spot, deep in thought. Her mind drifted away from the pastor's sermon, wandering into a world of possibilities beyond the confines of her sheltered life. While the pastor was teaching about faith and commitment, Shelly was thinking about her friend Amaya, who was very different from her in many ways. Amaya was impulsive, free-spirited, and didn't appear to be constrained by a rigid upbringing. She was a big party girl, always seemed to be having fun and living a life that Shelly could barely imagine for herself.

On the other hand, Shelly was a devoted Christian who respected her religion and adhered to its principles. But she couldn't help but feel uncomfortable about the high expectations placed on her. Since the burden of her mother's laws sometimes felt oppressive, Shelly yearned for a taste of the freedom that her friend Amaya enjoyed so easily.

It wasn't that Shelly wanted to completely reject her background or her faith. No, she sincerely loved God and appreciated the morals that her family had taught her. She couldn't help but imagine how life would be like outside the high walls of her sheltered existence. The siren's call drew her for possibilities outside of her small environment.

Shelly's heart ached as she watched her friend post pictures of herself having fun on social media. She knew that her friend was living her best life while she was stuck at home, unable to even go to her friend's house. She couldn't help but wonder how different her life was from Amaya's as she sat in that church pew. She felt jealous as she thought of the adventures Amaya had while she was bound to her mother's stringent guidelines. She believed it was unfair that Amaya could access nearly anything she desired while she felt confined in her own life.

Shelly's parents had a love marriage. Her mother had been just 18 when she became pregnant with Shelly, and despite the challenges they faced, her parents had gotten married, driven by love and a sense of responsibility. However, ironically, years later, their marital life had everything except for love and regard for each other, and Shelly has been witnessing it since she was a child.

Shelly knew nothing about the harsh realities of street life. But she could not fight the gnawing curiosity that drove her toward the unknown. With each passing day, her yearning to leave her comfortable life and take charge of her own destiny grew stronger.

While Shelly was a nerd and smart girl, she couldn't know that her desire for freedom would lead her down dangerous pathways and teach her valuable life lessons.

Chapter Two

"Tangled In Temptations"

(Two Years Later)

Shelly stood on the stage with pride, surrounded by her classmates, all set to welcome her freedom that she assumed would come with this milestone as she is about to graduate. She is now 17 and legally viewed as an adult by the state. She could barely contain her excitement thinking about all the freedom and fun she can have now.

She thought about all the parties she had missed out on, all the dates she hadn't been allowed to go on, and all the adventures she hadn't been able to have. She couldn't wait to finally be able to do whatever she wanted, whenever she wanted.

She maintained an impressive 3.4 GPA as she got ready to graduate and go to college, proving her commitment to her academics. After years of preventing her from participating in numerous activities, her parents finally decided it was time to give her some freedom.

Recognizing her maturity as graduation approached, her parents let her participate in typical teenage activities. Shelly could now go to the mall, hang out with friends after school, and attend more social events. The additional independence, though, needed to be more for Shelly. She continued to hunger for more, especially after Amaya told her that her boyfriend Rob was hosting a party on the upcoming weekend.

Shelly couldn't help but envy Amaya's life because it seemed full of adventure and excitement. Shelly's protected background stood in sharp contrast to Amaya's, who was raised in a home with only one parent, and she was responsible for taking care of her younger siblings while her mother worked two jobs. She adopted a rebellious lifestyle, sneaking out to parties, using drugs, and drinking excessive amounts of alcohol out of contempt for her circumstances. Amaya was also brilliant, but she was caught up in her own lifestyle because of her resentment towards her situation at home and with her mother and her living situation and how she has to grow up faster.

In search of a release from her own limitations, Shelly discovered herself pulled into Amaya's world. So she snuck out to join Amaya's weekend party, where she ran into a guy named Antonio Valentine, Rob's friend. Shelly decided not to participate in the party's crazy activities, which included underage drinking, smoking, and drug use because she was unfamiliar with it. She stayed to hang out, enjoying the excitement of what was happening in the atmosphere.

Unable to control her urge for freedom, Shelly continued sneaking out for a couple of weekends until Patricia, her mom, caught her. Now, her mom was furious this time, and she grounded Shelly after seeing her sneaking back into the house.

Shelly's mother is a dedicated and strict parent who firmly upholds her Christian faith in her parenting style. Being a teen mom, she was determined to protect Shelly and keep her out of trouble. She married at a young age and shared her husband's faith-based values, taking on the role of the disciplinarian for Shelly.

Though she is a loving wife, she often feels unnoticed and unappreciated by her husband due to his frequent absence. Being a working mother adds to her emotional exhaustion, and sometimes, she may display a bad temper or frustration when dealing with Shelly's behavior. She sees her daughter as spoiled, entitled, and sheltered, which adds to her concerns and sense of responsibility as a parent.

One day, worried about her daughter's security, she

attempted to bring up the matter with her husband, Joshua, the senior deacon of their Christian congregation, but he appeared aloof and indifferent, dismissing her worries. The neglect in their marriage and communication increased Patricia's anger and animosity towards Joshua.

The distance between Shelly's parents widened as the days went by. Patricia perceived Shelly's bad behavior as a result of Joshua's lack of guidance and control. As a wife and mother, she couldn't help but feel neglected and forgotten. She felt the growing distance between her and her daughter and the strains in their marriage, which weighed heavily on her heart.

Patricia's severe parenting style was motivated by her love for her daughter and her beliefs. Still, she couldn't eliminate the worry that Shelly was making poor decisions without Joshua's supervision. On the other hand, Joshua had little time for his family because of his commitments to the church. He spent most of his time servicing the church and running church organizations and programs due to his head position as a deacon. As a result, Patricia must step in and play the bad cop with Shelly to teach her discipline. Shelly's father makes up for the time he is not around by lavishing Shelly with gifts, but he neglects to deal with her increasingly rebellious behavior. He only takes charge of issues he feels are essential and not what is important to both him and his wife, causing problems in their marriage and bringing a rift between Shelly and her mother. Patricia fretted more as her kid grew older because she believed she required her husband's help and presence to get through these crucial years of their daughter's life. What she hated the most was the fact that Joshua had no clue that his marriage was on the rocks and that she was unhappy and was considering divorce. And now that Shelly was of age, Patricia was worried that she might be beginning to make bad choices as her father was not around to help with the discipline.

Patricia longed for her husband's support, while he only wanted to hear the good things about his daughter without recognizing what was really going on at home.

However, little did he know that what was coming next would shatter their family forever.

Chapter Three

"The Rebellion Move"

Time rushed on, and another year passed by. Shelly, who is now 18 years old, was about to graduate from high school, a huge life event. A burst of resolve was felt as years of academic work came to a close. She began to feel more like an adult, with a desire to carve out her own path and leave her mark on the world. Her desire to experience life's ups and downs on her terms was stoked by the excitement of independence. Shelly radiated a blend of pride and eagerness. The ceremonial cap and gown marked a rite of passage, symbolizing the bridge she was crossing from adolescence into adulthood. With the tassel poised to shift, she embraced the future with arms wide open. The stage was set for a graduation ceremony and the next stage in Shelly's life. Now, she was ready to be an adult. She was ready to be on her own and make her own decisions.

With the growing age, Shelly's defiance against her parents also surged as she continued to slip away under the cover of night, drawn into the deceptive world of parties and companionship. One evening, while at a gathering with Robin and Tony, they extended an offering of rebellion: a joint and a beer. Amaya, too, encouraged Shelly to embrace the forbidden, urging her to indulge in the drugs and alcohol that had become synonymous with their nights out.

Shelly's surprise was evident – Amaya's participation in such activities came as a shock to Shelly. The realization that her closest friend had been keeping this facet of herself hidden left Shelly questioning the true nature of the world she had become a part of. Amaya confessed that she had chosen not to expose this side of herself to Shelly earlier, fearing how her friend might perceive her. But as their paths converged into this wild world, Amaya felt it was time to be honest, to unveil her true self.

Peer pressure weighed heavily on Shelly's shoulders, tugging her closer to the edge of a precipice she had long resisted. The drugs and alcohol that once seemed foreign now beckoned to her, promising escape and euphoria. With a mixture of fear and curiosity, Shelly couldn't help but give in. She devoured the substances that had become an integral part of her new life, and in doing so, a new normal was introduced into her days.

One unfortunate night, her audacity peaked. She entered her childhood house under the impression that she was subtle enough to dodge observation while in a high and drunken haze. But destiny had a different plan. Her father's harsh glare, filled with a mix of disappointment and rage, confronted her faltering figure. Her rock, the guy she had always looked up to, stood in front of her as an embodiment of power.

While he was aware of the rumors and whispers that his daughter was deviating from the course, he had planned for her, witnessing Shelly in such a condition shocked him. The carefully cultivated college dreams now appeared to fall apart like delicate paper in the wind. His wife's concerns, once brushed aside, now resurfaced with undeniable weight. Shelly's actions were more than teenage rebellion; they were proof of her spiraling out of control.

Shelly's father gazed at her with a sad heart and an iron will, trying to find the right words to cut through the fog enveloping her. The emotion that had been simmering for weeks eventually surfaced. He was not just her father; and he was a husband who needed to rebuild trust with his wife, who had been right all along. The dynamics of their family had shifted, disrupting a delicate balance.

On the other hand, Shelly stood before her father with hopeless eyes shiny from alcohol. She was confident in her ability to use her charms, as she had countless times before, to influence her father's choice. She nevertheless tried to speak, but her remarks were ignored. The serious resolve of a man who had reached his breaking point had taken the place of her father's waning patience. His stern eyes and cold words broke her world's heart because she was daddy's girl, and she's never seen her father react in this manner.

She tried to plead with her father. She tried everything she possibly could, but her father was not having it like. He was fully fed up with Shelly now. There was no opportunity for negotiation left. She was to depart and find another route. The house, which was once a haven, now served as a sad reminder of the life she had abandoned.

Shelly felt a pang in her heart like she had never felt before. She could sense the distance between her current situation and her former way of life growing as she stood on the verge of a new chapter that would be shaped by her decisions and the results of those decisions. She was no longer a carefree teen; instead, she was a young adult standing on the other side of the door of her house with nothing but a bag of guilt and an uncertain future.

Chapter Four

"The Budding Romance"

The darkness of the night reflected Shelly's tornado of feelings as the city's pulse echoed through the streets. In a desperate attempt to get help, she dialed Amaya and Antonio with trembling fingers and told them about everything that happened that night.

The invitation to Antonio's flat was a ray of hope, a break from the storm that had forced her from her home.

Antonio's apartment had a hazy odor of smoke that she instantly smelled as she entered, reflecting the kind of life he led. With a knowing look, Antonio handed her a joint promising consolation and comfort from the internal strife. An unsaid connection that went beyond words was provided by the shared ritual, which involved dancing with the ethereal tendrils of smoke.

While listening to Shelly about how her dad overreacted, Antonio followed the pain-stricken creases on Shelly's face. He was fully aware of the gravity of her father's disappointment and the echoes of broken trust. A sense of kinship developed between them as they began to build a sense of connection with each other.

Amid the confusion, a surprising relationship developed. Her acceptance of Antonio's invitation to remain in his flat turned into more than just a brief reprieve; it signaled the start of an unknown trip.

As weeks passed, Shelly and Antonio struggled to draw a fine line between friendship and something more. A silent romantic connection grew between them as they exchanged laughter, whispered confessions, and sly glances. Shelly, who was once lost in doubt, discovered herself firmly immersed in Antonio's company after being pulled to the warmth and the safety his arms provided.

She deliberately chose to stay with Antonio for an indefinite period of time; it was a step into the adult world she had long desired. Their lives were effortlessly entwined, and each day was characterized by a feeling of cohesion that softened the sharp edges of their past. While Antonio traveled his own less common but no less true road, Shelly balanced her career, a piece of her former existence.

Shelly accepted Antonio's reality for the sake of their newfound love, despite it deviating from the standards she had previously upheld. The shadows that covered his days and nights as a drug dealer became a part of her world and were welcomed without condemnation. She accepted him without conditions or hesitation for who he was.

Shelly now felt she had finally taken control of her life's course with a place to call home and a partner by her side. She felt as though her choices and actions were expressions of her independence. She had no idea, however, that this new chapter of love and acceptance was only the beginning of a storm that would make her question her choices.

The journey with Antonio had only just begun, with Shelly being unaware of the impact Antonio was going to have on her life.

Chapter Five

"The Beginning of Domestic Violence"

A year into their relationship, Antonio got caught by the police trying to sell drugs to undercover officers. Shelley was at work when he called her from jail, trying to explain what had happened and what he needed her to do. This was the beginning of Antonio's toxic, narcissistic behavior. He made himself out to be the victim, claiming that he had been stopped for no reason and that Shelley needed to come and get him out of jail. Shelley felt sorry for him and bailed him out.

At last, Antonio was released from jail, but he was unhappy. He needed to get more drugs to replace the ones he had lost, and he needed Shelley's help to do it. He knew that Shelley's regular job would not bring in enough money fast enough, so he came up with a plan. He told Shelley to call her old friend Amaya, who worked for Rob (Antonio's old friend and fellow drug dealer.) Antonio explained that Amaya got paid daily, and he thought that Shelley might be able to get a job with her. Shelley had not talked to Amaya in over a year, but she was so deeply in love with Antonio that she agreed to call her.

Shelley was hesitant to call her friend Amaya after so long, but she knew she needed to talk to her about the job opportunity Antonio had mentioned.

With a deep breath, Shelley pressed the call button. The line rang a few times before a familiar voice filled her ear. "Hello?"

"Amaya? It's Shelley," she said, her voice tinged with a mix of nervousness and relief.

There was a moment of silence, then Amaya's voice brightened. "Shelley! Oh my god, it's been so long. How have you been?"

Shelley felt a lump in her throat as she spoke. "I've been... okay, I guess. Listen, Amaya, I actually called because I heard from Antonio about a job opportunity you might have."

Amaya's tone grew curious. "Oh, really? What kind of job is he looking for?"

"He mentioned that you have a job where you get paid daily," Shelley replied.

Amaya's laughter was warm and genuine. "Ah, that job. Yeah, I do have something like that, but it's not your typical nine-to-five, Shelley."

Shelley's heart pounded as a mix of curiosity and apprehension bubbled within her. "What kind of job is it?"

Amaya hesitated for a moment before she spoke. "It's dancing, Shelley. Exotic dancing, to be precise. I've been doing it for about a year now."

Shelley's breath caught in her throat as the words sank in.

Exotic dancing. The very thought sent a shiver down her spine. "Dancing? Like... at a club?"

"Yeah, exactly," Amaya confirmed. "Look, I know it's not something everyone would be comfortable with, and I totally understand if it's not your thing."

Shelley's mind raced, conflicting emotions battling within her. The idea of dancing in such a way was foreign and intimidating, but the desperation in her situation nudged her toward considering it.

"Amaya, I... I need money, and Antonio said this might be a way to make some fast."

Amaya's voice turned sympathetic. "I get it, Shelley. Times can be tough, and I've been there too. Just remember, it's not an easy job, and it's not for everyone. Take your time to think it over."

As Shelley hung up the call, she stared at her phone, her thoughts a whirlwind. Shelley was surprised and upset. She couldn't believe that Antonio would suggest that she do this kind of work. She told Amaya she would get back to her after she had a chance to discuss it with Antonio.

The next night, Shelley told Antonio about her conversation with Amaya. She told him that she was not interested in becoming an exotic dancer, and she was very disappointed in him for suggesting it. Antonio tried to justify his actions by saying that he was just trying to help her make money, but Shelley didn't buy it. She knew that he was just trying to take advantage of her.

Shelly's refusal to do the job made Antonio furious. He flipped out and started choking Shelley, almost choking her to death.

As Antonio's angry outburst resonated throughout the small, darkly lit room, Shelley stood there, her heart pounding. Her mind was a jumble of uncertainty, terror, and rage as her breath came in ragged gasps, and tears filled her eyes. She had no idea the man she loved could turn into this monster capable of such brutality.

She clenched her throat, still feeling the pressure of Antonio's hold, and stared at him in a mixture of shock and amazement. The person who had once pledged her love, safety, and happiness had changed into something terrifying and unrecognizable. Her hands trembled as she wiped away the tear that had rolled down her cheek.

Antonio's fury appeared to pass just as swiftly as it had come. He took a step back, his eyes reflecting his own shock. In stark contrast to the chaos that had just taken place, the silence in the room grew oppressive and dense. He slowly extended his hand as if he wanted to touch her or offer an apology, but he appeared to change his mind and let his arm fall back to his side.

His voice quivered as he sputtered, "I... I didn't mean to," "I'm not sure what happened to me, Shelley. You simply don't comprehend the stress I'm going through. I wanted to avoid hurting you."

As she listened to him speak, Shelley's heart began to flutter. As much as she wanted to think that this was a one-time mistake brought on by stress and desperation, she was unable to erase the vivid memory of his hands being around her throat and the horror she had experienced.

Her voice was scratchy from the pressure on her neck as she croaked out, "Antonio," barely audible. "I didn't fall in love with this individual. I can't... This can't go on, I promise."

Antonio's eyes flittered with anguish and understanding. His voice was begging as he took a cautious step forward. Please, Shelley. I apologize. I swear I won't let it happen again. I can't let you go because I love you so much.

His comments caused her heart to ache. She was being torn apart by internal strife. She recalled the precious times they had had together, the laughing, and the dreams they had created. But the violence that hung over them made that love, which had previously been so pure and lovely, feel corrupted.

She could see the manipulation and toxic influence he had started to exercise over her as she looked into his eyes. She was reminded of his first phone call from prison and how he had concocted the story to make himself the victim as a warning. She was forced to take notice of the warning signs, the evidence of his narcissism and manipulation.

While all these thoughts jumbled up in her mind, Shelley took a step back, moved away from him, forming a distance between them. She continued, her voice shaking but resolute, "Antonio, I need time to think."

"I can't simply move on from what happened. We must discuss this, but I require some privacy."

The expression on Antonio's face twisted between despair and desperation.

"Please, Shelley. Stay with me. I swear I'll do better. I'll get support."

However, Shelley was familiar with these guarantees. She had read about and heard about the cycle of abuse, but she never imagined that she would become caught up in it. Even though it hurt, she realized she had to put her safety and well-being first.

She said it again, this time with more sternness, "I need time to think, Antonio." I must determine what is best for myself."

With that, Shelley turned and left the room, leaving a broken relationship and a shell of the person she had once known. She realized that her adventure was far from over as she stepped into the crisp night air. The path ahead was uncertain and filled with difficulties she had never anticipated encountering.

Shelley lay in bed, staring at the ceiling. She couldn't sleep. She was still thinking about her argument with Antonio the night before. He had asked her to take up a job as an exotic dancer, and she had refused. He had gotten angry and had started choking her. She had managed to escape, but she knew that he would not let this go easily.

She knew that she had to make a decision. She could either

take up the job and stay with Antonio or leave him and start a new life. She didn't know what to do. She loved Antonio, but she couldn't live with the way he treated her. Neither of them knows what the next morning will bring.

Chapter Six

"Making Difficult Choices for Living"

As Shelley spent the night thinking while looking out at the city below, the sky began to lighten. By that time, she knew what she wanted to do. Part of her decision was influenced by fear and a soft corner for Antonio. While she never wanted to opt for this career path, she couldn't say no either. The love for Antonio outweighed her own happiness. She knew that she would never be truly happy if she stayed with him, but she also knew that she couldn't leave him. She was trapped in a cycle of abuse and addiction.

Finally, Shelley took a deep breath and dialed Amaya's number. She had been thinking about this for days, ever since Antonio had suggested that she become an exotic dancer. She knew that it wasn't something she wanted to do, but she also knew that she needed the money. Antonio had been unemployed for months, and they were barely making ends meet.

"Hello?" Amaya's voice answered on the second ring.

"Hey, it's me, Shelley," she said.

"Hey, Shelley! How are you?"

"I'm okay," she said. "I'm calling about that job you mentioned."

"Oh, yeah," Amaya said. "I'm glad you called. I was just about to give up on you."

"I'm in," Shelley said. "I'll start tomorrow."

"Great!" Amaya said. "I'll see you then."

Shelley hung up the phone and felt anxious, completely unaware of what she was signing up for. However, there was a sense of relief as she had decided, and she was determined to see it through.

The next day, Shelley showed up at the club early. She was nervous, but Amaya greeted her and calmed her nerves. She showed Shelley around the club and introduced her to the other dancers. Shelley's first shift was slow. She was nervous and didn't know what to do. But Amaya was there to guide her, and she slowly started to relax and enjoy herself.

By the end of the night, Shelley had made a lot of money. She was surprised at how much she enjoyed the attention and the money. And she was even more surprised at how good she was at it.

Shelley started dancing at the club regularly. She quickly became one of the most popular dancers. She loved the attention and the money, and she was good at it. But the more she danced, the more she felt like she was losing herself. She started to feel like she was just a commodity, an object to be bought and sold. She began to use drugs to cope with the emotional pain, and she soon found herself caught in a cycle of addiction.

Shelley's new life was beginning to weigh her down and break her spirit. The vivacious young woman who had previously fantasized about love and happiness now discovered herself caught in a cycle of negativity, addiction, and emotional upheaval. She stood backstage under the neon lights of the club, her heart heaving with need and despair.

So, after a year of working with Amaya, Shelley came home one night from the club drunk and without any money. The night had been slow, and she had spent most of her money on drugs in an attempt to cope with the fact that she had to be in the club. She also wanted to loosen herself up and cope with the lifestyle she was living.

The door creaked open, revealing a dimly lit apartment. The

faint scent of alcohol lingered in the air as Shelley stumbled inside, her steps unsteady. She closed the door behind her with a thud, her movements sluggish. Her gaze swept the room, landing on Antonio, who sat on the couch, his face contorted in anger.

"Where's the money, Shelley?" Antonio's voice was sharp, cutting through the heavy atmosphere.

Shelley's eyes flickered as she tried to focus on him, her thoughts muddled by the alcohol and the drugs she had consumed. "Money? What... What are you talking about?"

His jaw clenched, and he rose from the couch, his fists tightening at his sides. "You spent it all, didn't you? You wasted it on those damn drugs again!"

A bitter laugh escaped her lips as she swayed on her feet. "Oh, so you care about money now? But you didn't care when you asked me to do all this for you. You didn't care about me when you choked me, Antonio."

His eyes flashed with a dangerous mix of anger and frustration. "Don't you dare throw that in my face. You think I wanted to do that? You pushed me to it, Shelley!"

Tears welled up in her eyes as her emotions bubbled to the surface. "You pushed me into this life, Antonio. You made me do things I never wanted to. And now you're angry because I can't bring you more money?"

His voice grew louder, laced with venom. "I'm trying to provide for us, Shelley. I'm trying to make sure we have what we need. But you're too busy getting high and dancing for strangers to see that."

Her vision blurred as she took a shaky step forward, her voice trembling with a mix of rage and desperation. "I didn't ask for any of this. I didn't ask to dance, to be in this situation. And now you're blaming me for it?"

Antonio's face reddened, his anger boiling over. "You're the one who said you'd do it. You're the one who agreed. Don't act like this is all on me."

Shelley's fingers curled into fists, her nails digging into her palms as she struggled to hold back the torrent of emotions within her. "I did it for you, Antonio. I did it because you pushed me into it, because you made me feel like I had no choice."

He took a menacing step forward, his voice a harsh whisper. "You always have a choice, Shelley. And now you're dragging us both down with your reckless behavior."

Tears streamed down her cheeks as her voice cracked. "I can't do this anymore. I can't live like this, like a puppet dancing to your tune. I won't let you destroy me."

Antonio's nostrils flared, his fists clenched at his sides. "Oh, so what? You're just going to leave? Go ahead then. See how far you get without me."

Shelley's gaze locked onto his, determination burning in her eyes. "Watch me!"

The space that had once felt like heaven now seemed suffocating to her. The reality of the situation began to dawn on her. Shelley was sure this relationship could not last long. She had to do something to escape her situation, but she was uncertain how she would do that.

Chapter Seven

"Escalation of Domestic Abuse and Financial Burdens"

Shelley was hurt and angry by Antonio's accusations. She felt like he was blaming her for everything wrong in their relationship. While working at the club, Shelley's mind wandered to Antonio's hurtful words as the music's bass reverberated through the walls. The irony that the guy who had forced her into this world was now accusing her of mismanaging the money was too much for her to ignore. She replayed the contentious conversation in her head, her eyes stinging with tears.

She attempted to gather herself by wiping a stray tear from her cheek and taking a deep breath. She had suffered both physically and mentally over the past year. The pull of the attention and the money was a perverse means of escaping the reality she had come to loathe, but it was only a short-term solution, a band-aid over the wounds Antonio's toxicity had caused.

She stepped into the backstage area, her thoughts cut short by Amaya's voice.

"Hey Shelley, how are you doing?"

With a strained smile and trembling voice, Shelley nodded. "Yeah, I just... have a lot on my mind."

Amaya put a hand on Shelley's shoulder, and her countenance relaxed. If that's not what you want to do, you are not required to do it. I am aware that, lately, life has been difficult for you.

Shelley appreciated Amaya's compassion, but a simple discussion couldn't calm the desperation that had settled down deep within her. Driven by a desire to flee her reality, she had found herself imprisoned in a world she had never intended to visit.

Shelley feigned ignorance, "I... I don't even know what I want anymore," she acknowledged, her voice breaking. Simply put, "Everything is so messed up."

Amaya tenderly held Shelley while casting a sympathetic glance her way. We'll work things out, promise. Just keep in mind that you have options, alright?

But Shelley thought the possibilities were limited. She had the impression that her circumstances were the strings on a puppet. She had forgotten her identity and her goals. The use of narcotics, dancing, and fake attention were all attempts to dull the agony and regain some measure of control over a world that had gotten out of control.

One night, Shelly's footsteps faltered as she entered her apartment, sensing a gripping tension in the air. She hesitated in the doorway, her heart pounding as she saw Antonio slouched on the couch, a half-empty bottle of alcohol by his side. His bloodshot eyes locked onto her, blazing with rage and intoxication.

"What took you so damn long?" he slurred, his words heavy and laced with bitterness.

Shelly's voice quivered as she tried to diffuse the situation. "I was just finishing up at work, Antonio. I didn't expect you to be here."

"Of course, you didn't." He sneered, his lip curling into a malicious grin. "Off dancing for those losers, aren't you?"

"No, Antonio, it's not like that. Please, just listen to me," Shelly implored, stepping cautiously closer.

But he was beyond reason, his anger spiraling out of control. "Listen to you? You're a liar, Shelly. Always have been."

Tears welled up in Shelly's eyes as his accusations cut into her, reopening wounds she thought were healing. "I'm not lying. I love you. You're the only one I care about."

He shot up from the couch, stumbling as he advanced on her. "Love me? Ha! You're a joke."

"Antonio, please, you're drunk. Let's just talk this out," she begged, her voice shaking.

He didn't seem to hear her, his face contorted with anger. "You're probably with someone else right now, aren't you? Sneaking around behind my back!"

Shelly's heart raced, fear tightening its grip around her. "No, Antonio, I swear..."

He cut her off with a shove, sending her stumbling backward. "Shut up! I'm sick of your lies!"

Her back hit the wall, and she felt the cold fear crawl up her spine. "Antonio, please, you're hurting me."

He ignored her pleas, his fists clenched as he loomed over her. "You think you can just get away with anything, don't you? Well, not anymore."

Desperation flooded Shelly's voice as she tried to reason with him through her tears. "Antonio, we can work through this. Please, let's just calm down."

But he didn't seem to hear her, the alcohol fueling his rage. His hand struck out, landing on her cheek with a sharp slap. "Calm down? You want me to calm down?"

Pain radiated through Shelly's face, a mix of physical and emotional agony. "Antonio, I love you. We can find a way to fix this. Please, just listen to me."

His response was a cruel laugh, as if her words were a joke to him. "Fix this? You're delusional. You're nothing without me,

Shelly. Remember that."

Before she could react, his fists began to rain down on her, the blows landing with a sickening thud. Shelly curled into herself, her arms shielding her face as the pain seared through her body. She sobbed, her voice a mix of pain and terror. "Stop, please! Antonio, stop!"

But the onslaught continued, fueled by his anger and fueled by the alcohol that had turned him into a monster. Shelly's world had shattered, her pleas falling on deaf ears as she realized she was trapped with a man who no longer saw her as anything but an object of his rage.

The next day, Shelly told her best friend, Amaya, what had happened. Amaya was horrified. She begged Shelly to leave Antonio. While Shelly knows that she needs to leave Antonio, she fears what he will do to her if she does. She is also afraid of being alone. She has been with Antonio for a long time, and he is all she knows.

On the other hand, she was also aware that living with Antonio was no longer an option as things with him only got worse. Antonio started cheating on Shelly with other women. He started spending all of his money on drugs and alcohol and stopped paying the bills. Shelly was left to pick up the pieces. She worked long hours at the club to make ends meet and was exhausted and stressed.

Shelly began to resent Antonio. She hated the way he treated her. She hated the way he made her feel. She knew she had to leave him, but she feared what he would do to her.

Chapter Eight

"An Unexpected Twist of Destiny"

It had been five years since Shelly and Antonio's toxic relationship had started. The once-vibrant spirit had grown accustomed to managing Antonio's unpredictable moods and tantrums. Over these years, she learned to manipulate his rage while treading carefully to avoid conflict.

Days stretched into weeks, and then those weeks grew into months, and Shelly found herself in a depressing pattern. Her soul was being drained by the continual need to please him, but she had gotten accustomed to their relationship's dark dance. Her eyes were no longer filled with joy; instead, they were now guarded and frightened, revealing the suffering she had been through.

She continued working at the club, but it was no longer a place of peace or momentary pleasure. The once-exciting neon lights now projected a melancholy hue, emphasizing the flimsiness of the existence she was entrapped in. Shelly intended to work there for the money and to survive in this dangerous world.

The topics of conversation with Amaya had changed, with hopes for a better future taking the center. They talked about leaving the club and creating a life free from the darkness they were enveloped in. Although Shelly's acceptance gave her reason for optimism, the idea of leaving Antonio remained a difficult task.

Then, as fate would have it, a twist of destiny threw her world into upheaval once again. After several weeks of sickness and doubt, Shelly's pregnancy was confirmed by a doctor, which caused both worry and a brief moment of elation. It was a ray of hope in a life that had seemed unendingly depressing.

With her heart brimming with worry and newfound hope, Shelly shared her news with Amaya.

"Amaya, there's something I need to tell you," Shelly began, her voice a blend of anxiety and anticipation.

Amaya looked at her with concern, sensing the gravity of the moment. "What's going on, Shelly?"

Tears shimmered in Shelly's eyes as she spoke, her words carrying the weight of her decision. "I'm pregnant, Amaya. I found out from the doctor. I can't believe it..."

Amaya's eyes widened, a mixture of surprise and empathy in her gaze. "Shelly, that's... that's big news. How are you feeling?"

Shelly's emotions surged, the weight of her circumstances pressing down on her. "I'm scared, Amaya. Scared for myself, scared for the baby. But it's also... It's also a ray of hope, you know? A chance to make things right."

Amaya's expression softened, her hand reaching out to rest on Shelly's. "You're right, Shelly. This is your chance to break free from all of this. To give your child a different life."

Shelly nodded, her determination resolute. "Exactly. I can't keep living like this, and I won't subject my child to it either."

Amaya's voice held continued support. "You're making the right choice, Shelly. Leaving the club, finding a new job – it's the first step toward reclaiming your life."

A fragile smile touched Shelly's lips, gratitude shining in her eyes. "Thank you, Amaya. I couldn't do this without you."

Amaya squeezed her hand gently. "We're in this together, Shelly. You've got my full support."

The news of her pregnancy renewed her motivation to provide her child with a life free from the bonds holding her back.

Shelly was excited to share this news with Antonio, hoping things might improve between them. However, little did she know that Antonio's reaction would shatter her into pieces.

"Antonio, I need to tell you something," Shelly's heart was racing with fear and anxiety.

"You're quitting the club?" Antonio's voice was sharp, his tone a mixture of incredulity and rage. "You think you can just walk away from that money? Do you have any idea how much I rely on it?"

Shelly's voice trembled as she tried to reason with him. "Antonio, I can't keep doing this. It's not just about me anymore. I have to think about the baby."

His laughter was bitter, laced with derision. "The baby? What baby? Don't make me laugh, Shelly. You've never cared about anyone but yourself."

Tears welled up in Shelly's eyes, her heart aching at his callous words. "Antonio, I'm pregnant with your child."

His reaction to the news of her pregnancy was a devastating blow. Shelly's heart broke as his denial echoed in her ears.

"Wait, are you kidding me? Whose child are you carrying in your womb?" His words were like daggers, stabbing into her vulnerable heart.

Shelly's voice shook as she tried to hold back her tears. "Antonio, how can you say that? You know we're the only ones involved."

He scoffed; his face twisted with disdain. "I've seen the way you look at other guys, Shelly. Who's to say this isn't just another one of your little games?"

Anger surged within her, but fear held her back. "You know this is yours, Antonio. How can you be so cruel?"

Cruelty seemed to fuel him, his anger growing more explosive. "Cruel? You want to see cruel, Shelly? You have no idea."

Shelly's heart raced as she watched his temper spiral out of control. The emotional abuse escalated his words like daggers that cut into her very soul.

"I won't let you ruin my life with your lies!" Antonio's voice thundered through the room, the atmosphere charged with toxic energy.

Shelly felt the weight of his rejection pressing down on her, a crushing reality that made her question everything. She was burdened not only by the pregnancy but also by his ruthless dismissal of her situation.

Shelly's emotional and physical health deteriorated during the course of the days. She fell into a state of despair due to the combination of her pregnancy hormones and the gloom of her circumstances. She struggled with the knowledge that she was now battling for the innocent life developing inside her as much as for herself.

Chapter Nine

"The Escape"

After weeks of procrastination, Shelly finally applied for a job at her previous employer. She couldn't be an exotic dancer anymore. She needed a new income stream to support herself and her unborn child during her pregnancy. She knew that getting a stable job would also help her get away from the hell that Antonio had created for her. But even as she took this step towards a better future, she couldn't help but feel a pang of guilt and remorse. She looked at herself in the mirror, staring at her own reflection, trying to recognize the girl she had become. She was no more like the girl she used to be. She was distressed, unwell, and, most importantly, she was alone. While looking at herself in the mirror, the room felt suffocating as she realized this was not the place she should be. She was frustrated and betrayed. She questioned herself, "What am I doing with my life?"

She should have been happy to hear she was being rehired at her old position, but instead, she was overcome with feelings and memories she had buried deep inside. The familiar line of the Lord's Prayers echoed in her head, bringing back memories of her younger years and their innocence. She found herself saying the prayer over and over again, turning to the words she clung to as a little girl for comfort and direction.

Once again, Shelly turned herself close to God and began to include prayer in her daily routine. She found peace and comfort in God's words. The daily practice of prayer created an opportunity for reflection. Shelly's thoughts were lost in the maze of her life, going over each action she had performed, each decision she had made, and each error she had made. Her parents' memories started to become clearer. What she had once perceived as strictness and coldness, she now began to understand as tough love, a desire for her to become her best self.

A feeling of enlightenment swept over Shelly as she saw herself assuming the role of parent. Her past fragments, which had appeared torn and painful, were suddenly coming together. As she stood on the verge of embarking on a similar journey herself, she recognized that her mother's protectiveness was nothing, but an armor woven with love.

Shelly's relationship with God became stronger every day. She was raised with a strong sense of faith, which helped her guide her path amidst the darkness that had enveloped her life. She had the strength to face the harsh reality of her marriage to Antonio, thanks to her spiritual reawakening. Because of this newfound courage, she was able to make the decision to leave Antonio behind for good and start fresh.

Six months flew by, and with each day, Shelly fortified her once-lost connection with God. Now, she felt herself strong enough to finally leave her toxic boyfriend, Antonio, and start a new chapter in her life.

It was a long night, Antonio was out with his friends, and Shelly was alone at home. The silence of the house was deafening, broken only by the sound of Shelly's heart pounding in her chest. She knew this was her chance. This was her chance to escape from the prison she had been living in for so long.

Shelly hurriedly packed her belongings, her hands shaking with a mixture of fear and excitement. She had to hurry. She didn't know how long Antonio would be gone, and she didn't want to give him a chance to stop her.

She took one last look around the room that had been her prison for so long. The walls were bare, the furniture was old and dusty, and the air was stale. She could still see the bruises on the walls where Antonio had thrown her against them. She took a deep breath and turned away, determined to never look back.

It was 3:00 a.m. in the morning when Shelly took a cab to the train station. She sat on a bench, waiting for the next train to arrive, her belongings piled beside her.

Shelly was both excited and nervous as she stepped outside into the night. Her familiar life, which was intertwined with Antonio's comfort and anguish, was being left behind. Her heart felt lighter with each step she took away from that location, as if shackles were being gradually removed.

The path was clear, but the destination was uncertain. Shelly decided to live the life she deserved and choose herself. Although the path ahead was blurry, it was hers to take it.

And just like that Shelly set out on her journey to freedom, which would put her to the test, show her true strength, and take her to a place where the scars of her past could finally mend and where she could begin again.

Chapter Ten

"The Doorway of Second Chances"

Shelly's gaze remained fixed on the worn, scuffed floor of the train as it rumbled along the tracks, the rhythmic clatter mimicking the tumultuous thoughts that churned within her. Her hands instinctively cradled her swollen belly, a tender reminder of the life growing inside her. Each passing mile was an imagery of the uncertainty that lay ahead as it was framed by the train's windows.

Shelly was pregnant and had nowhere to go, but she couldn't go back to Antonio. She thought about her parents' house, but she felt guilty about leaving them so long ago. She knew they would welcome her with open arms, but she was afraid of their reaction to the news of her pregnancy.

As the train's journey drew closer to its destination, a quiet determination began to build within Shelly. The faces of her parents, their warm smiles from long ago, flashed vividly in her mind. The vision of their home, nestled amid familiar trees and dappled sunlight, emerged like a piece of heaven, calling her weary soul.

With a deep breath, she made her choice. She would go to her parents' home, once again. The idea that had seemed daunting and distant before now felt to her like a lifeline. The train's brakes hissed as it came to a stop, and with her heart racing, Shelly got off it.

The cab ride from the station felt like an emotional rollercoaster for Shelly. With each passing mile, her heart raced faster, and the feeling of going closer to her childhood home intensified the turmoil within her. As the vehicle pulled up in front of the familiar house, a wave of nostalgia washed over her.

She stared at the door, her palms damp with nervousness.

Five minutes ticked by as she wrestled with her inner feelings and emotions.

Finally, a deep breath filled her lungs, and with it came the courage she sought. Shelly's knuckles rapped gently against the door, the sound resonating through the air and mingling with the fluttering of her heartbeat.

From within the house, the silence was short-lived. Footsteps approached, and the door swung open to reveal her mother, her eyes wide with disbelief.

"Shelly?" her mother's voice wavered as if unsure if her senses were deceiving her.

Shelly met her mother's gaze, her own eyes brimming with a mixture of fear and hope.

"Hi, Mom," she whispered, her voice carrying the weight of years gone by.

Her mother's features shifted rapidly from astonishment to joy, a cascade of emotions playing out on her face. Without a moment's hesitation, her arms enveloped Shelly in a warm, familiar hug.

"Oh my dear, my dear," she murmured, her voice trembling with emotion. "You're back."

Shelly's eyes were wet with tears as she stepped back slightly, the smile on her mother's face a mixture of happiness and confusion. Her father appeared in the doorway, drawn by the commotion, and his eyes widened in disbelief at the sight of his daughter standing before him.

"Is that really you, Shelly?" her father exclaimed, his voice a mixture of amazement and uncertainty.

A bittersweet smile graced Shelly's lips as she nodded, her gaze shifting between her parents. "Yes, Dad, it's me."

Her father's brows furrowed, his eyes falling to the

noticeable swell of her belly. Questions and emotions swirled within him.

"Shelly, what...?" he began, his voice trailing off as he struggled to find the words.

Shelly took a deep breath, her heart pounding in her chest.

"I have so much to tell you," she said softly, her voice carrying a weight of honesty and vulnerability. "Can I come in?"

Her parents exchanged glances, a silent conversation passing between them. Then, her mother nodded, her eyes softening with understanding.

"Of course, come in, sweetheart," she said, her voice gentle and inviting.

With each step into the house, the atmosphere shifted from uncertainty to warmth. The living room, a place that held countless memories, seemed to welcome Shelly back as if she had never left.

While Shelly was back home, she was no longer the same girl who had left five years ago. She was now a mother, with a baby to raise. She was also working full-time to support herself and her child. But despite the challenges she faced, Shelly was determined to get her life back together.

She enrolled in college and started taking classes, even though it was difficult to balance her studies with work and childcare. She also joined a support group for single mothers, where she found support and advice from other women who were going through the same thing. Church had become a big part of her life again as Shelly had rejoined her childhood church and even became a member of the choir there.

Christmas was around the corner. It was going to be over a year since Shelly had left Antonio.

Shelly sat with her daughter nestled in her arms, the warmth of the fireplace painting an idyllic scene of togetherness. The soft laughter of shared stories and the aroma of holiday treats hung in the air, spreading serene vibes of familial love. They were all gathered around the Christmas tree, singing carols and decorating the house, when there was a knock at the door.

Shelly's heart skipped a beat, her gaze darting towards the door. Her parents exchanged glances, their expressions mirroring the mix of curiosity and caution that Shelly felt.

With a tentative breath, Shelly approached the door, her daughter's curious eyes following her every move. The doorknob felt cool beneath her touch, and as she swung the door open, the scene that greeted her was no less than a nightmare.

There, against the backdrop of the winter night, stood Antonio, a reflection of his brutal past. It's been over a year since she left him.

"Shelly," he began, his voice a mix of hesitance and yearning. "I... Can I see our child?"

Shelly was stunned. She couldn't believe that Antonio was standing there, after all this time. She had thought she had escaped him, but now he was back.

Made in the USA
Monee, IL
04 November 2026

67382568R00026